Penelope

PENELOPE

Penelope Thinks While Homer Writes

Julie M. Whitaker

Parlor Press
Anderson, South Carolina
www.parlorpress.com

Parlor Press LLC, Anderson, South Carolina, 29621

© 2024 by Parlor Press
Printed in the United States of America
S A N: 2 5 4 - 8 8 7 9

Library of Congress Cataloging-in-Publication Data on File

978-1-64317-490-7 (paperback)
978-1-64317-491-4 (pdf)
978-1-64317-492-1 (ePub)

2 3 4 5

Parlor Press, LLC is an independent publisher of scholarly and trade
titles in print and multimedia formats. This book is available in
paperback and ebook formats from Parlor Press on the World Wide
Web at https://parlorpress.com or through online and brick-and-mortar
bookstores. For submission information or to find out about Parlor Press
publications, write to Parlor Press, 3015 Brackenberry Drive, Anderson,
South Carolina, 29621, or email editor@parlorpress.com.

Contents

Index of First Lines

To Michael, Shannon, and Brendan

Foreword

Who Is Penelope?

Penelope, faithful wife of Odysseus, mourns for twenty years as her husband fights wars, confronts monsters, or succumbs to the odd god or goddess. Given Homer's preoccupation with the adventures of Odysseus, it is intriguing to imagine Penelope's slant. The epic style is objective, formal, and less concerned with what the character thinks than what he or she does, but one must wonder, how does Penelope feel as she lives alone in her palace in Ithaka while Odysseus roams the world? What annoys or delights her? What are her hopes and fears? What makes her angry or nostalgic? What does she want?

In *The Odyssey* Penelope is the queen, but as her husband has been absent for twenty years, the kingdom has fallen into chaos. Her home is overrun with rude and ambitious suitors looking to benefit themselves through marriage to her. That ready excuse for their presence gives them full opportunity to exploit the situation. Sheep and cattle abound in Odysseus' kingdom and the wine is good. Her son has become a young man but without the image of his father to guide him. Penelope is clever. She puts the suitors off by saying that she must weave a funeral shroud for her father-in-law, Laertes. She weaves by day, but by night she unravels that shroud. Then she is betrayed by servants of her own household who tell the suitors of her trick.

After twenty years, Odysseus does return to Ithaka, but in venturing into his home, he is both wary and wise. He comes disguised as a beggar so that he can see for himself who has been faithful and true, and who has betrayed him. Even Penelope does not know that the begger she meets and speaks with is Odysseus, though she does have some inklings. Finally, the hero Odysseus and his son Telemakhos confront the suitors in battle and kill them all. While this climactic confrontation takes place, Penelope, touched by Athena, sleeps quietly upstairs in her chamber.

On waking Penelope descends to find the suitors gone, destroyed by the strange beggar and her son, and the hall transformed. The Beggar? Touched by Athena, he seems to be Odysseus. But only after testing him with secret of their bed, an olive tree, does she embrace her longed-for husband.

Penelope

Introduction

In Homer's *Odyssey* we see the plight
Penelope endures. Her man is gone
and she a wife alone stands 'midst the blight
of rude unruly suitors, some who fawn

for favor of her hand, her wealth, her bed;
but others grab what bread and wine they find
kill goats and cattle, gluttons, till they're fed
then drunkenly reel home, the future's blind

Poor Penelope. How trapped she seems!
For twenty years, with tears and cries profound
she weaves a shroud by day, her secret dreams
set down with warp and woof; by night unwound

    Perhaps she weaves a tale of passions grand,
    but then destroys its thread with tight-clenched hand.

Her Plight

> *"Sing no more*
> *this bitter tale that wears my heart away."*
> —Penelope
> I.391–92

High in her room, she weeps—
alone, her loss worth more than twenty years
Twenty years before he rose from out her bed
Twenty years before his shadow crossed the doorsill
Twenty years before the light grew dim
as he set sail for Troy to fight
for someone else's wife

That night the Pleiades shone bright
with points of light in darkness
there to guide them, warriors all, to Sparta
and he in their lead
The shadowy ship slid over the black water
a ghost eclipsed by the horizon

Her tears began that night
And when the brutal morning light
hit shining tables, silver basins
golden cups, their richness mocked her
She looked out on an empty hall
a hearth of wispy ashes
and she wept

But in the desert of her heart, a light
glows still refracted by her tears. He lingers
there transformed by twenty years, an image
fitted to her mind's design
Her warmth is his

Now, the words of Phemios sing
through the hall and echo up the stairs
recalling Troy, that bitter tale, once more—
a tale without conclusion for Penelope
As she descends, a veil shines across her cheeks
shines as eyes should shine unveiled by tears

The Loom

"Does she intend to keep us dangling forever?"
—Antinoos, a suitor
II.123

What a woman! Her trickery's beyond us
Weaving is the women's art and craft
It keeps them in their rooms, out of the way
until we want them. It keeps them quiet too

Here's what she did to fool us, clever bitch
Hiding behind her grand loom, she wove a tale
to free her from our pleas, a tale laced up
with duty and religion and country honor's due
"Poor Lord Laertes! No shroud for him in death's defeat!
It is not right that he should be without
a tribute to his life when darkness calls."

She argued well, and we, fools taken with her charms
put our hopes on hold until the shroud
should be complete—since there were feasts, and music
in the meantime—Why not?

But she dissembled to the end
From dawn till dusk, she wove high in her hall
Such diligence, devotion to her cause!
How could we know her dark deceit of all?
At night by light of torches she unwove
what she had done that day, such cunning! Then
with morning's glow, she would begin again
to weave the shroud

Three years she carried out her fraud, and we
suspected nothing until a maid brought news
of her deception. We caught her in the act
destroying lines of linen that shimmered in the glare
Hah! No more could she fool us

                              And finish it
she did, as we looked on

7

Anger

"I wish this were the last time they came feasting,
courting me or consorting here! The last!"
—Penelope
IV.733–34

In the manor house the revelry goes on
The men carouse and plot their pillage

Penelope, alone upstairs, can do
nothing to stop it
The suitors gather for her beauty
but from the corners of their eyes
the hall looks rich and generous
The feasting's fine, the games are good
the camaraderie of like-minded men holds all

Her anger flashes out
"Courting or consorting!
Wolves devouring all before them—
They eat my good son's fortune at their leisure.
I want them gone!"
she calls out to the stone walls of her room
"gone . . . gone . . ." calls back, soft mockery

Metallic anger echoes in the air
but impotence hangs heavy there with no
release. The image of Odysseus
looms large in her imagination
How small they are, those men
compared to one more like a god
Grief folds her in familiar pain

Betrayal

"Why has my child left me?"

—Penelope
IV.758

"Your son is gone."

The news assaults her, deadening her soul
Motionless, she stands
The instant holds a rosy face, fat baby toes, a laughing boy
a dreaming boy who gazed beyond the walls
a figure like his father's
head and hands and glinting eyes
The shock of loss she can't control drains all sensation
'til with a wail of pain she sinks upon the floor
her sorrow strong upon her.

Where can she turn? Who is to blame? How could
he leave, he too? Her child is not her own.
Her servants have betrayed her, left her out
The oldest one especially—sent him off
with grain and wine and a promise not to tell.

What comfort from the soothing words of servants?
"Trust to the gods. Pray to Athena. Hope."

Refreshment comes with bathing and with prayers
The words assure, the language hovers in the air
Stark words: "Save my son!"
A cry of pain resounds

A Dream

The goddess sent this dream to Odysseus's house . . .
IV.850

With tortured thoughts, she tossed
'til sleep crept in to still her turning
into that calm
Between the noisy world
and the quiet inner core
the phantom image of her sister rose
Athena's answer to her anguished cry

"He will return unharmed."

What longed-for words
came from Iphthime's cloudy mouth!
Her sister's words so cool, so soft, so strong
Yet even those, she heard distrustfully

"Why have you come, why now?"
Defiantly, "Am I told to grieve no more?
My son is gone,
a boy who knows no conflict and no council."
Despairingly, "He is my only son,
one whom I raised in sunshine and bright air.
But violent waves and thunder now surround him.
For him I cry
more than his father."

But comfort comes with ghostly declaration
Iphthime speaks once more

"Trust Athena. She will be there for him."

A Mother's Son

"At home indeed your mother is, poor lady,
Still in the women's hall. Her nights and days
Are wearied out with grieving."
                    —Eumaios, a loyal swineherd
                              XVI.46–48

He was a boy of golden curls and laughter
who trailed behind the workers asking questions
or came to me with presents, shells and flowers—
So soft his little hand, so bright his eyes!
I weep for that lost child

He was ungainly as he grew
but most endearing
His limbs stretched out embracing air about him
With newfound strength, he vaulted over fences
and ran the rounds with speed unprecedented
and always with a shine of eyes, delighted
in sunny days or evenings' tales repeated
I weep for that lost boy

No father led him. Only raucous fools
who ate and drank his fortune in these halls
were his companions
Against their sway, he dreamed, confused
alone, unknowing yet
how strange it was

How proud I felt. How sad—
His growth, my joy, my loss, my hope—
His voice grew large and filled the room demanding
that they leave. He was a man
I grieve for that lost son

Mixed News

She knew now
they plotted her child's death in her own hall . . .
XVI.499–500

Medon, the herald speaks:
"The suitors have cast off to follow him, your son—
A chosen group of twenty strong, the best
among them, chase after Telemakhos.
He's marked. They're out to get him, kill him.
I heard their plot."

In her high room she crumples to the floor
her sister's visionary words receding
Such comfort there—
"He will return unharmed."
How, how . . .
She weaves the image of those words in blue
tinged gold with hope
Weaving, weaving, what else can she do?
Each thread forestalls despair of too much thinking
Odysseus, and now Telemakhos, husband and son
both beyond the shores of Ithaka
beyond her touch, her care, her warmth

In the halls below, each night loud voices
clanging goblets, raucous laughter echo
up the stairs. How hateful are the sounds!
They shout disgrace for Lord Odysseus
and murder for his son
How hateful are those oafs who eat and drink
and lust for her while plotting death
for the one she loves!

She lashes out with passion and despair
"Evil, evil! You are malignant, spreading
chaos with your beastly appetites!
How can you be so cruel, deceitful?
To plot against my son, betray the very kingdom
that has sheltered you and yours?

Can you forget the welcome offered
to your father, Antinoos?
No more of this, no more!"

Quick to respond with lies and honeyed phrases
Eurymakhos takes over
Denying all, they are unmoved
and she returns to weep

Then second hand, the information comes again
A crier's voice fills streets and halls with joy:
"He has retuned! Your son is back unharmed."

Son's Return

"Mother must see me there, with her own eyes,
or she will weep and feel forsaken still . . ."
—Telemakhos
XVII.9–10

"Telemakhos! My son, my son!"
and with him light of morning—
There! He steps across the sill
How large he is! What grace,
the echo of his father

My arms enfold a man. Yet still a boy—
My own, my own—I thought him lost—
The curling hair, the shining eyes, the eyes
that look beyond—

"How could you leave without a word
to me, without a hint? I feared your death—
swallowed by the wine dark sea or caught by
wicked men. Oh, now you're here! What joy!
What have you seen? What shores, what news have you
brought back? What of your father, anything?
Tell, oh tell!"

How far away he is. His eyes glance off
my face, his words are strange.
He says, "Not now, go bathe, go pray—
Pray for revenge."

Warm water, clean linen, a prayer—
in my chamber away from the hall
I am alone again with only maids to call

Impatience

Then softly she withdrew
to bathe and dress her body in fresh linen . . .
XVII.71–72

This narrow room confines me
The quiet of the walls creates a prison
with maids as guardians of my loneliness
My loom stands vacant, vacant as my heart—
In winter when the fields are barren gray
and fold into the sky without a seam
to tell the viewer, "This is earth and this is sky,"
so my emptiness is like my loom
pale, unvarying. No blues, no reds
dance from right to left and back again
No tales fill in its frame
and here I am again, waiting, waiting

What can I do but wait and spin more thread
multi-colored, passionate, to fill another spindle?
My loom stands vacant, vacant as my heart—

Like nervous fingers drummed on tabletops
I twist the fibers forming threads of woolen
yarn. Perhaps there is a start, a tense
beginning, just unfolding in the hall below

I'll go there—

I sit apart, I lean in silence watching
as my son and his odd guest consume
the food before them. I ask no questions
'til their hunger and their thirst are satisfied

My fingers twist the threads in steady rhythm
The roughness of the touch consoles me
'til I speak

"What news? How can I wait and weep
another hour? It's been too long!"

New Hopes

In silence
across the hall, beside a pillar, propped
in a long chair, Telemakhos' mother
spun fine wool yarn.
                          XVII.120–23

Nestor of Pylos, Menelaos of Lakedaimon, and Helen
Those names recall a time flushed with light
before Odysseus set sail, before the loss of twenty years
I was young and handsome then with trust
complete. I loved him totally
sure that each day held a sweetness soon to follow
Our son was young, his body soft with baby fat
his tongue untuned except for cries and giggles

Paris, Helen, Menelaos, and Troy—
those names came crashing down between us
crashing like the waves that bore him out to sea
the years since then made moist by my tears

Our son Telemakhos now speaks
His voice, how changed! Dark echoes of his father
as his tale unfolds: Odysseus held captive
on an island? And in a sea nymph's thrall?
He can't depart? He has no ship, no oars?
But he's alive! Dare I have hope? Take care—
Such rumors have no certainty at all

Theoklymenos breaks in, my son's odd friend
His words are strong and certain. Odysseus is here
on the island? It cannot be
His words were prompted by desire to please
I dare not think what might be—yet what joy!

If it were so—to him I'd give rewards
"Such gifts, such love for you should this be true!"
a promise from my heart

The Sneeze

Mother and son now heard
Theoklymenos, the diviner...
XVII.189–90

How strange that prophecy, how like a dream—
Odysseus returned to this, his home!
But words are easy. Signs are what I need

From the hall below the noise of revelry
resounds. How dare they! Opportunists!
Free to feast and drink and loll about
they take what they can get without a
thought of what they do, the hateful beasts!
They cannot even give a crust
to that poor beggar wandering through
I curse them from my heart
Would that Odysseus were here!

A sneeze! What's that? Telemakhos has sneezed
a blasting sneeze both grand and eloquent!
The gods are laughing, and I share their glee
How right that was, how clearly I see the
absurdity of great and small alike!
Would that such a blow would clear the hall
deal death at once to all who gorge themselves
at our expense

The Stranger

Have you not brought him? Why? What is he thinking?
—Penelope
XVII.757

The air's alive. My head is light
Something has changed
A stranger there, across the hall—

What brings him here? Where has he traveled?
What lands has he seen? What news might he bring?
And why is he untended?

The air's alive. My head is light
Something has changed

He begs, and yet his stance suggests
nobility and wisdom broad
He should share the plenty of our table
To leave him there amongst the suitors
rabble that they are, intent
on food and wine, whatever they can take
is shameful. It will not do—
and I would speak with him
Go. Call him!

The air's alive. My head is light
Something has changed

I long for tales of different shores—
shores Odysseus might know
shores far from here. Oh, dare I hope?
He may have met Odysseus
Go call him!

The air's alive. My head is light
Something has changed

Realization

And now a heart-prompting from the grey-eyed goddess
came to the quiet Penelope
                                            XV111.200–01

                        As I wake
I'm laughing still with strange delight
My nodding off was soft as a summer breeze
that kisses the cheek and ruffles up the hair
It is absurd, but why not go below?
What can I lose?
Why not torment the boys a bit?
They cannot have me—I have other plans
and gifts are always welcome, even useful

I feel a glow, a queer excitement, something new
I glide into the hall. There's space about me
none dare cross. They only gasp and glance
at one another. I look at them and laugh
behind my veil

Their flattery is grand
my beauty and my majesty—indeed!
They'd take me home for theirs, proud of possession
proud of mastery, caring not at all
that I detest them
Fools they are and weak in reason—They!
The cream of all the local isles!
I'll scold them as a mother would
for they deserve no better
and I deserve much more

Her Challenge

"How galling, too,
To see newfangled manners in my suitors!"
—Penelope
XVIII.341–42

They flatter me. Well, let them
Such words may well
remind them of their place—and mine
Beside Odysseus they look like beasts
whose appetites define their acts
I, marry one? Impossible!

Yet it is true. My son is grown and years
have passed since Lord Odysseus set sail
I'll taunt them with the possibility
of marriage though I will have none
I'll join the game. Their greed consumes
our household. I'll have something in return

"Where are your manners? Most who court bring gifts,
but you forget yourselves in revelry,
in beef and wine consumed, through you bring nothing
to complement the stores of this, my home.
If you would have me as a wife,
show your desire."

They look ashamed as well they should—
and wondrous gifts they bring. Pins, brooches
golden necklaces and clustered jewels on earrings
gleam in their hands. I smile and nod
though in my heart, I weep for one long gone

.

First Meeting

*"Now he shall talk
and listen, and be questioned."*
—Penelope
XIX.118–19

On soft sheep's fleece the stranger sits before me
A man of humble means, a man of woe
his face is lined, his shoulders bent, but dignity
surrounds him. And to my questions he responds
with care. His words are gentle praising me
and in his praise he places me within
a kingdom such as I have known, a kingdom
rich with wheat and fruit and springtime lambs
Oh, I wish it were as in my past
before Odysseus set sail for Troy!

My name he knows and honors, and he sees
my plight. The suitors there below, who court
as they consume, who flatter as they eat
and drink fine wines not offered, who make my home
their own. And I, the while, can only waste
with hopeless longing for my lord's return

The stranger's air invites my confidence
To him I say more than I mean to say—
Such sympathy unlocks my tongue, how odd!

I tell him of my trick to fool the suitors
my weaving and unweaving. I tell him how
the maids betrayed my secret to those churls
I tell him that a marriage soon awaits me
and that I can fend it off no more

He looks at me with double seeing eyes
as if he knows already what I say
as if my phrases could belong to him
I catch myself and question him instead

The Stranger Speaks

. . . then carefully Penelope began:
                                    XIX.123

"Now tell me, sir, what is your history?
Where have you wandered? What lands have you seen?"
"Oh, tell me of Odysseus," I want
to cry, but I hold back
I'll learn the stranger's past

Reluctantly, as though to recollect
brings pain upon him, he speaks
He hails from Krete, from Knossos. Ah!
The youngest son of King Minos, a prince!
Yes, that quality of strength, the royal
bearing—of course, of course
He tells of home and family, of his isle

Then quietly, he says "Odysseus—"
I cannot breathe. The name rolls from his tongue
like music or like poetry foregone
He knew my lord, was host to him at Knossos
twenty years before!

Tears bathe my cheek. How limitless they seem
I weep for twenty years gone now without him
I envy time the stranger spent near him
My hunger for a word recalling what he said
or how he stood or what he wore
consumes me. Yet can I trust this man?
Are his words true?

"Ah, tell more! Some proof that what
 you say is so, some detail of his dress
or of his look."

Truth and Lies

"Friend, let me ask you first of all:
Who are you . . .?"

—Penelope
XIX.124–25

His words are studied. Each is picked with care
but soon a picture rich with life fills out
It is Odysseus that he describes
down to the shining brooch
with hunting hound and dying deer in gold
the lustrous shirt, the purple cloak that I
set softly on his shoulders, weeping then
as I weep now—though then I did not know
how desolate the years ahead, how empty
of my lord. Today, these tears are painful
drawn from deeper wells of memory
grown cloudy with the time. Precise and piercing
every aspect of his person fills my mind
as if he might step forth incarnate, here

I hold my head. It will not be. Cruel vision!
It is too close. I cannot hope that he
will ever step across the sill into
my arms. Oh God, to touch that cloak, that brooch
to hold Odysseus. I must not dream

"And you, kind stranger, gifted
with such memories, are like warm sunshine.
You touch a time long gone. Leave off—
Odysseus will not return to this his land.
You say he is alive and near at hand—?"
But rumors such as these I push away
He will not come.

New Friend

Now hearing these details—minutely true—
she felt more strangely moved . . .
                                        XIX.295–96

The stranger's voice is powerful, dramatic—
It sounds the center of my soul with tones
from other times. Familiar feelings rise
as if a melody unheard for years were sung again

I'm filled with wonder at the ease with which
I greet him, welcome him and wish him well
He, a man hard-pressed and poor—and yet
his tales awaken pictures of lost time

No stranger now. He is a friend, new-found
and far above the fools who snore below
None of their grasping greediness, he'll find
a refuge here. I'll offer him a bath
soft rugs, repose from all the trials behind him
and when the morning comes, he'll rise refreshed

For twenty years he's been away from Krete
For twenty years, for twenty years—the sun
and moon have taken turns in time
For twenty years, Odysseus is gone
and age comes on, for him, for me, for all

To Odysseus

. . . she wept

for Odysseus, her husband

XIX.697–98

Oh, how I long to see you, talk with you—
Odysseus. Your painful name resounds
deep in my soul. Oh, hear and understand
Our son has come of age, and I must part
from this my home, Odysseus, and yours
I cannot hope that you'll return again

No more the grace and power of your stride—
No more the kindness brimming form from your glance—
No more the high excitement in the air
as you begin to speak, with flashing words
You spun such tales, precise for each occasion
with time and place and colors fitted out
so all who heard were in your thrall, enchanted
by the stories that you told. No man
can hope to match your honeyed tongue

You were a good shot too, with pleasure high
in acts of war, your gestures grand and deadly
Your bow was like an instrument which only
you could play. You bent it, strung it, then
displayed your strength and skill in shooting
singing arrows to the mark precisely
through the axe heads lined twelve in a row

If I must leave my home, my son at last
I'll join with him who takes the bow and bends it
to his will, then shoots an arrow through
as you have done with ease—but I will curse should one
be equal to the task

The Night Before

*Wakeful again with all her cares, reclining
in the soft bed, she wept and cried aloud . . .*
XX.65–66

My quiet room, my solitary room—
Here on my single bed I lie with fear
inside my heart—a pain intense. My breath
comes fast as if I stood upon the edge
of nothingness, a chasm black and empty
yawning there, where I must step with no
return in reach. I'll say those words. "A contest
will be held and I'm the prize." O hateful!

Long have I pushed back their grasping hands
long repelled their queries with good reason
My child Telemakhos was young, defenseless
but now he is more than boy—a man
a man grown strong and independent
and I have no excuse. I cannot
bear to think on my departure from this home—
into the arms—
I cannot bear to think

Let death come now a shaft from Artemis
that stops my heart. In Hades I might see
Odysseus, a shadow of himself
I know, but he would shine in darkness.

Even now, I see him here before me—
How grand and tall and glorious he is!
He stands before his troops—as in the past
a waking vision, oh—too sharp. Too real!

The anguish of this night will smother me
and dawn tomorrow bring my darkest day

Suitors Last Supper

. . . while in the hall
the suitors roasted mutton and fat beef
on skewers, pulling off fragrant cuts;
XX.305–08

This day unfolds full grimly. There below
the suitors sit stuffing their maws with meat
Their talk is raucous and their laughter mad
Like pigs, they snort and gurgle, gulping wind
between their shouts of wild hilarity

Telemakhos does nothing, a host or no—
His words are muffled, but his stance—
like a coil ready to spring forth
And yet he has no force against their number
By his side the stranger, my new friend
whose graceful movements echo in my mind
something I can't recall, something now lost—
He too is prey to their gross energy

Which one of them must I allow? Which one
will win my hand? I'm filled with loathing
and a deep despair at what I will
propose—a contest to replace my lord—
Oh, no—I cannot move without some help
from someone greater than myself. Athena, come
or Artemis, again I call on you

Resolve

Upon Penelope, most worn in love and thought
Athena cast a glance like a grey sea
lifting her.

XXI.1–3

I know what I must do. Each step I know—
The bow—I'll bring it forth, the bow so precious
that Odysseus chose not to take it
when he left for Troy. And axe heads. Yes
those too. I'll test those men contemptible
though if one should succeed—I cannot think

Down the stair and cross the hall I'll go
and find the storerooms filled with bitter treasures
treasures of my lord, Odysseus
I have the bronze door hook, my key, its ivory
handle smooth against my palm
With it the heavy door will yield

How far the room seems, there across the way—
I touch the oaken door and feel the grain
of fine wood worked to silken smoothness

                                   There,
there is the slot. I place the hook within
Yes, yes. Just so. The bolt breaks loose
and now the door swings open with a roar
of hinges rubbing one on one. I breathe
perfume of linens packed with rosemary
and thyme, and touch the chests, and run my hands
across the bars of gold and bronze and iron
There, before me hangs the bow encased
in leather finely worked

                            I lift it down
and unlatch the case—and ah—the shining bow!
He touched it here and grasped it there, and pulled
the string. Odysseus's bow I hold
Ah, damn! The tears again, the tears for him—
Odysseus—whom I have lost

The Contest

Then back she went to face the crowded hall
tremendous bow in hand . . .
                                        XXI.66–67

Look at them, the suitors grouped before me
The hall is crowded with their hulking shapes
Unruly fools, they nudge and knock each other
their leering eyes upon me where I stand

as if I were an object to be bought
Despicable! But I will speak

My voice is steady and my words are strong
I tell them I have witnessed their behavior
their plunder of my house has sickened me
In their pretense of courting, I see only
their excuse to eat and drink, to carry on
at no expense. Lust for the marriage bed
the cause they share, should justify their acts?
No, no. If they would have my hand, my life
let them compete

I take the great bow now and hold it forth
I challenge them to bend that bow and string it
then shoot an arrow through the twelve axe heads
that like ship's ribs line the mound beyond
I promise that should one of them complete
the task, with him I'll join in marriage, though
I leave this home, my bridal joy, forever

They look at me with wonder, then glance sideways
They blink their eyes and clear their throats and cough
in their discomfort. At least they feel some shame
or is it fear, perhaps, of failure?

                              Cowards all—
A witness now, I watch as they proceed

They Try

>   *. . . clods,*
>   *they go to pieces over nothing . . .*
>   XXI.92–93

Sneering Antinoos mocks their aversion
to the task. The pretense of his words—
as if he would protect me from the sad
memories—rings hollow in my ears
His arrogance belies such fine intent

Telemakhos! Why do you laugh, then brag
about my excellence and urge the men
to try their hand? My son! I am your mother
Yes, I watched you grow from crawling babe
to golden striding man. I'll soon be gone
Have you no care for that?

Ah! You, Telemakhos, will try the bow
you too. You can't resist a contest
a chance to prove your strength.
I watch with wonder as you lean back
into the bow to bend it. Once. Then twice
three times, you pull the string almost to
the tip, but with the fourth, the closest yet
you stop. Behaving like a boy again
you shake your head and giggle, give excuses
for ineptitude, then turn away
Are you your father's son?

Leodes now steps up at Antinoos'
urging. He is too delicate, a mystic
without spine. He can't succeed, not he
And others follow one after another
They push and pant and groan. The bow won't bend
Then more contenders try. It will not budge
With quiet joy, I watch their futile efforts
they quit and stumble back into the herd

Even Eurymakhos, with all his might
and guile, can't force the bow to bend
or loop to catch. His parting words ring true
What shame for them their failure brings, poor fools
And I rejoice with silent laughter

The only one I fear has yet to try—
Antinoos—ambitious, strong and rotten
with conceit. Now he speaks out

He will postpone the day? Not even try
until tomorrow? Clever boy! Why spoil
the evening's feast? Defeat might cast a pall
Though that's not his excuse

But careful, now. My hopes stop short
I cannot see tomorrow

The Beggar and the Bow

'But let me try my hand at the smooth bow!
Let me test my fingers and my pull . . ."
—Odysseus
XXI.318–19

The stranger sits beside Telemakhos
he whose curious story gave me hope
he too would try the bow
He asks permission of Eurymakhos
and Antinoos as if they had the right
to say. His voice is humble, soft in tone—
and in my heart I wish him well

But Antinoos retorts, vile man—
as if he were the master of the hall
he throws out insults, threats, comparisons
and warnings dire. I am appalled and sickened
I shake my head in disbelief to hear
such base abuse of one who is our guest

I interrupt his tirade breaking in
to silence him. I cannot bear his words,
presumptuous and surly as they are
and I speak truly

                              "Let the stranger try.
Why not? He is no threat to you. Perhaps
you fear the competition of a man
who has no home, no domicile, one whom
I could not wed?"

Eurymakhos chimes in. Of course, it is the shame he fears, what folks
might say about them; they whose uninvited
presence darkens still Odysseus's hall
whose gross consumption of both beef and wine
whose raucous games, whose cowardly intent
continue year on year
They have no shame to lose

I say, "Give him the bow!"

The Son Takes Charge

"This question of the bow will be for men to settle,
most of all for me. I am master here."
　　　　　　　　　　—Telemakhos
　　　　　　　　　　XXI.396–97

Telemakhos, my son, breaks in scowling
and turns to me. His face is set, his eyes
flash glints of light and high excitement
tints his cheek. How changed he is!

His voice is low, intense yet loud enough
for all to hear. He makes a public
proclamation—not for my ears alone
though he addresses me with due respect

He would have me know: the bow and who
may try it is for himself to decide—not me—
nor any of the rabble in the hall—
as if he looks ahead to my departure
when he alone is lord and master here
　　　　　　　　　　　How changed he is!

He speaks to me with blunt authority
off to my room he'd have me go
back to my loom, my spindle, my maids—
away from the fray, the contest, and back
to my place high in my chamber apart
Men will decide, says he, about the bow

There is nothing I can do but go
I duck behind my veil to hide my hurt
but in my room, I tear it off and twist it
into knots, too hard to dab against
my angry tears. It twists and coils
like a snake, and I cry out

But then resignation settles in
I sink upon my bed, untwist the veil
and throw it on a stool. Oblivion—
Oh, yes! Give me the nothingness of sleep

One More Dream

". . . Some god sent her a drift of sleep."
—Eurykleia
XXII.483

"Nothing, I want nothing in my soul—
a blank emptied of feeling and design
Come silent sleep, and carry me away."

With that Athena touched her and she slept

She stood upon the door sill. The brightness of the sun
bathed the trees with gold and warmed the earth
It was a vision that called out. What longing
had she for the light of that bright scene!

As she stepped forth, a falcon flew from left
to right and right to left, his shadow
like a huge dark cloud, drained the luster
from the view, but when he folded in his wings
and landed near, the light returned

She spoke soft words and picked a bit of corn
from off the ground and held it out enticingly
The hawk hopped near, then fluttered, brushing wrist
and shoulder with a touch like softest silk
She stroked him, and he rubbed against her thighs
and nestled in her lap with calls and cries
She gathered him into her arms and wrapped
her veil about him tucking in his claws
and wings. She cradled him, caressed his head
With sweetness she was filled and light played
off her smile as she released him
shaking out her veil, but he would stay
She took a corner of the cloth and twisted it
then tied it softly 'round his neck

With that a voice rang out:
"Wake up, Penelope, wake up!"

News

"Odysseus is here! Oh, in the end, he came!
and he has killed your suitors, killed them all . . ."
— Eurykleia
XXIII.8–9

What noise! Oh, don't disturb me—
Odysseus is back? With what wild news
dares she break in upon me and destroy
my restful sleep, my dreams—my gentle dream—

Odysseus is back? She's mad or charmed
by some cruel god to rave without coherence
Odysseus is back, the suitors dead?
Poor, dear thing, she's lost her mind with age—
She can no longer grasp the dissolution
of this kingdom grand, nor bear to see
Telemakhos displaced and me alone
Her sympathy has pushed her to the edge

And yet, she says it's true. He has returned
and killed the suitors, all, with his son's help!
How could that be? How could one man—or two—
defy the power of that crowd of wolves?
Oh, joy! My tears are now more painful
than before. Dare I hope? Oh, tell me more—
How could that be?

No, no—her story is a fantasy
The suitors dead and strewn about the floor
Odysseys, triumphant, standing there
a lion fierce whose awful strength prevailed?
Not only that. The corpses are gone
the hall is cleansed, and he has called for me!
No, no—some god has meddled with her mind

Yet she insists that all is true. Perhaps
those fools have met their doom. Perhaps
their arrogance and greed were seen by a
divine who couldn't bear it and took steps
to do them in, a fate well earned. But could

Odysseus return just now? No, no—
Odysseus is gone. He'll not return

And she says she saw his scar,
his mark unique. Upon her life, she swears
that he is here, below. Some strange man, or god
perhaps—I'll go, descend the stair—

Uncertainty

"Let us join my son, though,
and see the dead and that strange one who killed them."
—Penelope
XXIII.92–93

My steps are measured, careful. First the
left and then the right. With each step
I mark a year alone, a year of anguish
longing for Odysseus, a year
of weaving and unweaving, a year
of watching our young son confused by all
the suitors, watching too, the disarray
of house and hall, a year enduring their crude ways—
and each step takes me closer to a man
who knows me not

A beggar, he appeared at first, the strange—
yet strangely close, familiar—and the bow—
what happened with the bow? And now the tale
the nurse has told me. What of that? With one
step more, I leave the stairs. The hall is there
before me. I cross the sill and stop
for I can go no farther

And there, across the way, the stranger stands
his figure painted with the gore of battle
his eyes cast down. The way he holds his head
the way his left hand rests upon his hip
his shoulders wide, his height—With grace he leans
against a pillar. Who is this man?
His figure fills my soul. I cannot move
with wonder

Telemakhos accuses me of coldness
He calls me cruel, unnatural to stay

apart from one whom he assumes I know
But twenty years fill up the space between us
I will have proof that he is ... who? Odysseus?
Who is this man—and who am I?

Now he speaks with Telemakhos
How like they are in gesture and in stance
I cannot hear his words—
Telemakhos responds respectfully
A nod, a smile, they're close in understanding
Both depart

                              The hall is empty now
but echoes of lost years reverberate
with bitter sounds, sounds I heard alone
Odysseus, a man who comes in rags
now would have my love as if no time
had passed? I will have proof, most certain proof!

The Test

"Athena
lent him beauty head to foot."
XXIII.176–77

Ah! The strange man is transformed
His robes are fresh, his hair glows golden
He pauses there beside the pillar
then seats himself, before he speaks to me

There's resignation in his voice. He calls me
hard, unfeeling, and he wonders at
my distance. How could I, his wife, remain
so cool on his return from twenty years
away?—as though his costume change would change
my heart. He says my heart is iron

Then, when he requests a separate bed
I speak. I look at him with longing, hoping
though my words are cool. I tell the maid
"Make up his bed, and place it in the hall
outside the bedroom built by Lord Odysseus."

With that, he breaks and lashes out at me
with raging words. "Who dared to move that bed?
How could they, saw it down or pry it up?
A god perhaps?" And I rejoice. He knows
he knows the secret that we shared!
The marriage bed grew from an olive tree
the center of our room. With his own hands
he cut and planed, and smoothed the trunk and branches
till the tree became our bed. What joy!
What joy! No man could move that bed!

I'm reeling now. With brimming tears
I run to him, embrace him, kiss his cheek
his lips. Odysseus is home at last!

Reunion

"Do not rage at me, Odysseus!"
—Penelope
XXIII.236

He's angry! His eyes are deep with pain
and I feel utter joy. He'll understand
With words I will console him, push away
the pain of twenty years apart

How could I trust him as a stranger
even though I knew his voice, I knew
his walk, I knew the way he held his head
his eyes? How many came before him
with one pretense or another, then stayed on
to eat the beeves and drink the wine

Proof. I needed proof, beyond all doubt
Our marriage bed, of course—
No one could know the secret of the bed
No man save Odysseus has seen it

Tears now fill his eyes. He weeps
as I have wept for twenty years
and holds me tight within his arms
as the fire lights hearth and warms the room
after a day endured in winter's season
so with his strong embrace my solitude
my silent loneliness dissolves into the air
He has returned. He holds me. He holds me

We are entwined with arms around
each other in disbelief and joy, with tears and laughter
and with this night
our lives are new

About the Author

Julie Whitaker was born in Salt Lake City, Utah. She attended Middlebury College in Vermont and New York University. A former dancer, she performed with the New York company of Alwin Nikolai. She taught English in Paris where she became acquainted with the composer Olivier Messiaen and his music. Because he had written a symphony inspired by her home state Utah, she arranged to have a mountain there named after him and a concert in his honor. On returning to New York City, she taught international literature at the Nightingale Bamford School. She is the coeditor of *Late Poems 1968–1993: Attitudinizings Verse-wise, While Fending for One's Selph, and in a Style Somewhat Artificially Colloquial* by Kenneth Burke. She has also written scripts for language tapes in French and German.

Photograph of the author by
Michael Burke. Used by permission.

www.ingramcontent.com/pod-product-compliance
Lightning Source LLC
LaVergne TN
LVHW010306070426
835509LV00030B/3499